The Coming King

Christian Drama Sketches for Advent and Christmas

PETER JACKSON

kevin mayhew

First published in 2007 by
KEVIN MAYHEW LTD
Buxhall, Stowmarket, Suffolk, IP14 3BW
info@kevinmayhewltd.com
www.kevinmayhew.com

9 8 7 6 5 4 3 2 1 0

ISBN 184417 805 6
Catalogue No. 1501032

Edited and typeset by Katherine Laidler
Cover design by Sara-Jane Came

Printed and bound in Great Britain

Contents

About the Author

Peter Jackson is a writer and editor living in Crowborough, East Sussex. From 1998 to 1999 he edited the monthly magazine *Celebrate* for the Church of England and is a lay preacher at his parish church. Interested in drama from an early age (a non-speaking galleon in Sheridan's *The Critic*) until the present (God in *The Mysteries*) he has also written for school and church groups, particularly the Rainbow Drama Group of All Saints, Crowborough. Ten of his sketches for children – including three Nativity plays – have been published by Kevin Mayhew as *The Star and the Stable*, and 50 sketches for church groups were published as *Acts of Faith* and *25 Christian Drama Sketches*.

Introduction

The twin themes of Advent give to this period of the Church's year a potent blend of expectation and rejoicing; we look for the return of the King before we find him in the manger. We look to the birth of the past and to the judgement of the future with the same mix of awe and wonderment.

These six sketches for Christian drama groups reflect aspects of each of these attitudes to Advent, from Mary and Joseph's pre-natal problems in 'Marriage Guidance' and the birth of Jesus in 'The Surprise Breakfast'; through John the Baptist's preparation for Christ's ministry in 'Clearing the Way' and the childhood, crucifixion and resurrection of Jesus in 'Reunion'; to his second coming in 'Sitting Tenants' and 'The King's Return'.

They can be played Sunday by Sunday from Advent to Epiphany, used as occasional productions with an appropriate sermon or talk, or run in their entirety as part of a special Advent evening, perhaps interspersed with readings and meditations. If this is your choice, then look at Ken Taylor's *Cradle of Hope: Meditations for Advent and Christmas* (Kevin Mayhew), which I have found particularly inspiring in writing these sketches.

At the heart of Advent is a child, a child who became a man such as this world has never seen; a man who suffered and died and rose again, to make the incredible journey from He Who Should Come to He Who Will Come Again.

As Ken Taylor puts it, 'He may take some finding, as shepherds and magi would testify, but he is worth the searching out.'

These sketches are intended to help those who are searching to move closer to their goal. Use them well.

PETER JACKSON

Using the Scripts

- **Bible sources** are given for each sketch where appropriate, as you may want to include a reading in the service, assembly or event.
- **Performance time** will give you a rough idea whether the sketch will fit the slot available.
- The **wording** of the scripts, although carefully considered for performance, is not sacrosanct and you are, of course, free to change names, places and characters, and swap male and female members of the cast if it makes the sketch more appropriate to your needs and resources.
- **Stage directions** are always from the actors' viewpoint.

Advent Sunday

Sitting Tenants

Advent brings not only joyful expectation of Christ's birth but also the biblical promises of judgement and separation at his second coming. With its echoes of an episode of *Men Behaving Badly*, this sketch is in no way intended to criticise a pizza/lager lifestyle; rather it provides a contemporary parable on the folly of leaving a decision about our relationship to Jesus until it's too late. Any cast can play this sketch but a 20s/30s age group would obviously be ideal.

Bible source 1 Thessalonians 5:1-11

Performance time Five minutes

Characters Danny – smooth, laid-back, fancies himself as tenant-in-charge
Debbie – bossy, selfish, bitchy
Jane – torn between being one of the crowd and siding with Ben
Tim – one of the lads; likes his lager and TV sport
Ben – quiet, thoughtful but determined; the keeper of the lease

Scene setter *The lounge/diner of 33 Woodthorpe Terrace. Table, chairs, TV (showing, if possible, motor racing with the sound off) and whatever else can be conveniently moved on and off. General air of untidiness and disrepair. Papers, books, cushions (at least three) and empty mugs scattered about. On table, pile of unwashed plates, empty wine bottles, lager cans, assorted cutlery. Tim, Danny, Jane and Debbie sit and lie around in various degrees of scruffy undress. Ben is off stage right.*

The doorbell rings off left. Everyone immediately comes to life and turns towards the door with a worried or puzzled expression, except Danny.

Debbie *(turning to others)* That's not . . . ?

Tim At this time of night? Can't be. *(pause)* Can it?

Jane *(getting to her feet, staring off left; slightly unhinged)* Oh, please no. I mean, we're not ready, are we? *I'm* not ready. Oh, please no!

Danny *(gets up and moves to the door)* Relax, children. It's the pizza man, isn't it? Remember I ordered the pizzas? *(waves his mobile phone)* Remember, Deborah? *(as he passes Debbie he waves the phone in her face and laughs)*

Debbie *(annoyed to have been worried; gets to her feet)* Yes, all right, Danny. We forgot, that's all. And don't call me Deborah!

Danny laughs and goes out left. Sound of door opening, talking, door closing with a bang. Meanwhile Debbie and Jane have moved across to the table and begun clearing a space.

Jane Look at this stuff. I can't believe we've let everything get in such a mess.

Debbie Give it a rest, Jane. You're beginning to sound like Ben. *(shouts at Tim who is lying on the floor reading the paper)* Tim! Get off your backside and shift this lot. *(Tim grunts)* Just do it, Tim!

Tim gives a resigned sigh, gets up and takes a pile of plates off right. The sound of breaking crockery.

Debbie *(loudly)* Oh, for pity's sake! *(she exits right with empty bottles)*

Sounds of Debbie and Tim arguing. Danny enters with five cardboard pizza boxes.

Danny You know, that front door's so warped it'll hardly close now. We ought to get it fixed. *(he puts the boxes on the table and Jane sorts out cutlery)*

Jane You've been saying that for months.

Danny Yes, well, there's no hurry, is there? He's not going to turn up without good warning. I'll get it fixed. *(sounds of arguing)* What's up with them?

Jane Oh, Tim broke some plates.

Danny *(laughs)* So what's new? Tim breaks things all the time. *(ticks off on fingers)* Plates, cups, fridge, toilet seat, kitchen window . . . that's just Tim. *(shouts off)* Come on, you two. Unless you want frozen pizza.

Debbie and Tim return, Tim carrying cans of lager and a bottle of wine which he puts on the table. The four take a pizza each and a drink and find themselves a space to eat. Tim sits glued to the TV.

Tim Yuk! This is disgusting! There's burnt anchovies all across one side.

Debbie Oh, don't be so childish, Tim. Take the other one. Ben won't even notice. He'll have his head stuck in that blessed lease as usual.

Tim, Debbie and Danny laugh. Tim walks to the table and changes his pizza.

Jane Well, I think that's really mean. Ben is one of us, after all.

Danny Ben is just a tenant, Jane. Nothing more, nothing less. And he's certainly not one of us!

Debbie Anyone would think you fancy him, Jane. *(Debbie, Tim and Danny laugh)*

Jane *(annoyed and embarrassed)* Oh, don't be ridiculous. *(she moves right and calls)* Ben! Pizza!

Ben *(off right)* OK. Down in a second.

Everyone returns to their pizzas, reading or watching TV at the same time. Ben walks in. He's casually but neatly dressed and carries a binder of papers. He sits at the table, opens the pizza box and begins to eat, reading the papers.

Danny *(with sarcasm)* Amazing what depths of enlightenment can come from reading a mouldy old lease. Don't you find that's so, Benjamin?

Ben continues reading.

Debbie *(with sarcasm)* Oh, don't bother him, Danny. He's been reading it for so long, it must be in Serbo-Croat . . .

Danny . . . or else he's a *very* slow reader. *(all except Jane laugh)*

Ben Well, it's neither actually, as you very well know. This explains how the house is supposed to look when the landlord arrives to inspect it. And at present *(looking round)* it doesn't meet the specification, does it?

Debbie All except *your* room, of course, Ben. All neat and tidy, is it?

Danny Oh, I'm quite sure it's pristine, Debs, pristine. *(to Ben)* What was that new emulsion you put on last month? Bootlicker lilac? *(Debbie and Danny laugh)*

Tim *(roused from the TV)* Bootlicker lilac. Are you sure? That's a weird name for a paint colour. *(Debbie and Danny laugh again)*

Debbie Just forget it, Tim. Go back to the motor cars.

Jane *(heated)* Just stop it, will you! Stop it! Why do we have to go on and on like this, always pretending. Of course Ben's right. This place . . . *(looks round)* . . . it's a tip.

Debbie And how would you know, Jane? Unless, of course, you've been able to compare it with the inside of Ben's bedroom.

Jane *(swings round on Debbie and grabs her by the shoulders)* Shut up, you freak! Just shut up for once! *(the girls grapple)*

Danny *(jumping up and pulling the girls apart)* Hey, hey, children. Calm down. Let's not fight among ourselves. Just because Benjamin is a weirdo, that's no reason to get upset.

The trio move apart and start to go back to their places. Tim switches off the TV, stands up and turns to Ben, can in hand.

Tim Anyway, how do you know that he's coming to inspect this place? Does it say so in there?

Ben *(stands and picks up the binder)* I don't know *when* he's coming. I only know that he *will* come. The lease says so. And we've got to be ready. It says here: *(he reads from the page)* 'The day of the landlord will come like a thief in the night.'

Danny Like a thief in the night! Excellent! Cue for a song. *(He picks up a cushion, holds it over his shoulder like a burglar's sack and starts to tiptoe in exaggerated fashion across the room, humming the tune that traditionally introduces drama and mystery – Dum, dum, dum, dum, daaaa, dum)*

Tim and Debbie roar with laughter and join in the second repeat. Ben and Jane stand looking on. Jane shakes her head. Ben holds the binder open in front of him looking straight ahead. The third repeat begins with Danny leading Debbie and Tim across the stage, facing left, all on tiptoe and each holding a cushion, all laughing. After the fourth 'dum' there are three extra loud knocks on the door and, if possible, a blaze of light from off left. Everyone freezes for a count of five then . . .

Blackout.

Second Sunday of Advent

The King's Return

Over the past 2000 years the sense of expectation of Christ's imminent return expressed by Paul to Timothy has been dimmed and at times eclipsed. People in general – and often Christians themselves – have 'turned away from listening to the truth and wandered away to myths'. This sketch obviously pays a debt to *The Lord of the Rings* and *Pilgrim's Progress* but also draws on many traditional stories – not least Jesus' own parables – where the rightful ruler arrives at last to depose the unjust steward and restore a misguided people.

Bible source 2 Timothy 3:14–4:5

Performance time Eight minutes

Characters Teachers of the Kingdom

Forktongue (M)
Gobbledegook (M/F)
All Equal (M/F)
Footloose (M/F)
Subversive (M/F)
Social Responsibility (M/F)

Council servants

Faithful – secretary (F)
Hopeful – security (M)
Truelove – catering (F)

Scene setter *A long table (or tables) set across the acting area covered in green baize or dark-coloured cloth. Seven seats face the audience, the centre one is a throne draped in red or purple on which is a large VACANT notice. One chair at the end of the table stage left for Faithful, another, slightly downstage from the other end, stage right, for Truelove, together with a tea trolley piled with crockery, biscuits, etc. The table is set out for a committee meeting with glasses, bottles of water, pads and pencils.*

The cast enter stage right, Hopeful leading. He mimes holding the door open for the rest. Forktongue is first and takes the seat stage right of the throne. The rest of the committee follow with Faithful and Truelove last. Hopeful closes the door and stands guard. During the meeting that follows, Faithful takes notes and Truelove pours and dispenses tea and biscuits.

Forktongue *(self-important; conducts the meeting briskly and without emotion)* Right. Everyone here. Good. Let's begin. Minutes of the last meeting, Miss Faithful.

Faithful gives a sheet to each of the Teachers, starting with Forktongue.

Forktongue *(reads from sheet)* Umpteenth meeting of the Teachers of the Kingdom. King's representative Forktongue in the chair. Present: Gobbledegook, All Equal, Footloose and Social Responsibility. Apologies from – er – Subversive; absent in – er – Much Carping. *(turns to Subversive)* Good holiday?

Subversive Hardly a holiday. International Tongue-wagging Conference. Still, it was most rewarding, thank you.

Forktongue Good, good. So, last time we discussed . . . *(checks through the sheet)* yes, yes, yes. That seems all in order. Everyone in favour? *(all murmur and raise their hands)* Excellent. I'll just sign . . . *(he does so)* . . . and we can get on. Agenda, Miss Faithful.

Faithful gives another sheet to each of the Teachers, starting with Forktongue.

Forktongue Matters arising. Ah, yes. Gobbledegook. You're reporting back on the Unspecific Language campaign.

Gobbledegook Indeed, yes, I have the honour of responding in that respect so to do. In the first place notwithstanding we have been able so to intricate and double-mean the kingdom's language that it is now perfectly possible to believe whatever one wants about any aspect of the kingdom – and vice versa.

Forktongue Excellent. And – er – All Equal, you have been working on the Kingdoms Come project.

All Equal We have indeed. With, I may say, a good deal of success. The idea that this Kingdom alone is not the only one but that many other kingdoms are equally good and true has found much popular support. Indeed, many of our own people have moved into the other kingdoms and have found that, of course, we all have much in common and there's little to choose between us. *(others agree, nod heads)*

Forktongue Splendid, splendid. Now, er, *(consults paper)* Footloose. You've been promoting the Say No to Marriage campaign. How's that working out?

Footloose Very promising or, should I say, very promise-breaking! *(laughter)* As you know, marriage rates have been falling rapidly and by umpteenth and twelve we hope to achieve a nil take-up. We've been producing these little lapel badges in the shape of a bent arm *(passes them round)* and they've proved very popular. *(confidentially)* As well as adding a substantial amount to the Teachers' Sabbatical Fund. *(murmurs of approval)*

Forktongue Very good news. *(examines badge)* I see. A little bent arm. And what's this slogan? Give marriage the elbow. *(amused)* I like it, I like it. Must give one to my – er . . . *(is lost for words and momentarily confused)* Yes, well, to continue. *(checks paper)* Ah, Subversive, have you anything to report back from Much Carping?

Subversive I think I can say that sustained progress is being made across the kingdom on the lines agreed at our last meeting. While we have not yet achieved total rejection of the traditional beliefs about the King and his origins, almost every aspect of the original charter has been discredited and we've introduced by-laws prohibiting the charter to be read in public or taught in schools. The idea that the King will ever return has been comprehensively refuted by leading articles in all the kingdom's broadsheets by the most eminent scholars.

Forktongue Well, that is most satisfactory news. Most satisfactory. *(he glances to his left)* Perhaps the day will not be far off when we can dispense with this chair altogether. On the other hand . . . *(he looks at it more intently and pats the seat; thinks for a second or two and is then brisk once more)* No, no, what am I thinking of? *(quietly to himself)* Not *just* yet, at any rate. *(slightly louder than usual)* Thank you all. That just leaves . . . *(looks at sheet)* Ah, yes, Social Responsibility. *(all sweetness and light)* How is it with you?

SR As you all know, caring for others in the kingdom was always done in the King's name and as a direct result of being one of the King's subjects. I believe there are several clauses in the – er – *(embarrassed)* charter about it – not, of course, *(false laugh)* that I have read any of that recently. *(murmurs of support)* Thanks to our planned campaign of official directives discussed at our last meeting, any association with the King has been almost entirely removed from hospitals, schools, prisons, rehabilitation centres, care homes and the like. Our citizens continue to do good works – but now for the right reason; it heightens their self-satisfaction.

Forktongue Absolutely right SR – I may call you SR? *(Social Responsibility nods)* Splendid. *(looks at sheet)* Well, it appears that all our agenda items have been covered by Matters Arising, so we are left with Any Other Business. So, anything further? *(as he reads out the names there is an appropriate shake of the head or 'no' or 'nothing, thank you' from the rest of the Teachers)* Gobbledegook? All Equal? Footloose? Subversive? And SR? Then without further ado I declare this umpteenth meeting of the Teachers of the Kingdom cl . . .

Faithful *(nervously)* I wish to raise a point of order.

Hopeful And so do I.

Truelove And me.

Forktongue *(spluttering)* You wish to raise points of order. That's completely out of the question. You are not Teachers of the Kingdom. You're merely – er – servants. Faithful, Hopeful, Truelove. *(he points at each in turn)* Nobodies.

Truelove Well, that's just where you're wrong, mister. We're citizens of the Kingdom. The King recruited us personally. And I'm not going to stand here, silent, while you rubbish the idea of doing good in the King's name . . .

Hopeful . . . and attacking marriage – which he instituted . . .

Faithful . . . and teaching that all kingdoms are the same as this one . . .

Truelove . . . let alone confusing the people so that they don't know what to believe any more . . .

Faithful *(finding her nerve and standing up)* . . . and, worst of all, making people forget who the King is and why he came to the throne and that one day he will return.

Forktongue Well, well. A very pretty set of speeches from a very pretty set of conspirators. I'm sure we have all been impressed by your misguided loyalty *(he grins at the other Teachers who laugh nervously)* but your moment of celebrity is now over – and you are going to be very sorry you opened your stupid mouths.

Hopeful Not quite. I've one more line to say.

Forktongue *(sarcastically)* And what can that be?

Hopeful *(opening the door)* His Majesty the King!

The Teachers rise, expressing shock, horror as they see the King. Their hands are raised as if to ward off a soul-piercing, penetrating beam of light. Hopeful, Faithful and Truelove also look to the King but fall on their knees and throw their arms wide open with the most joyful expressions. Everyone freezes for a count of five then . . .

Blackout.

Third Sunday of Advent

Clearing the Way

Next to Jesus Christ, one of the most well-attested names in the Gospels has to be John the Baptist; his birth, ministry and death are fully chronicled and his Advent credentials are without question. His imprisonment and execution at the hands of Herod Antipas can be seen to prefigure the trial and execution of his second cousin Jesus. This two-hander sketch is based on an imagined conversation between the herald of the Messiah and his worldly captor.

Bible source John 1:19-28; Matthew 11:2-15; Luke 3:1-20; Mark 6:14-29

Performance time Six minutes

Characters John the Baptist
Herod Antipas
A guard

Scene setter *A cell in the fortress of Machaerus, Peraea. John sits on a rough bench down-stage right, staring out towards the audience. Beside him are two blankets, spread on the floor as a bed, an empty plate and mug. If possible, a painted barred window on the back wall or supported on a tubular microphone stand. A decision will need to be taken on costume – first century or modern day. Both have their merits.*

Throughout the sketch Herod masks his uncertainty and inward fear of John with an approach streaked with spite and sarcasm. John remains calm and resigned to his fate throughout.

The sound of a lock turning off-stage left. Herod enters, followed by the guard.

Guard Do you want me to remain, Excellency?

Herod No. Leave us – but stay close to the door. *(the guard bends his head and exits left. Herod walks across to within a few yards of the bench and looks at John, who remains staring forward)* And how is the great prophet today? *(silence)* Not talking? Well, there's a surprise. I thought that was what you did best. Telling the people they were sinners, telling the Pharisees they were vipers, telling me I couldn't marry whom I liked.

John *(still looking forward)* I am not a great prophet.

Herod Are you not? I had heard you've been compared to Elijah, Elisha – even Isaiah.

John *(still looking forward, still calm)* Then you have been misinformed, Tetrach. Certainly I have been privileged to fulfil the words of Isaiah. *(stands)* I am the voice of one crying out in the wilderness, 'Make straight the way of the Lord'. *(sits)* But I am no prophet – merely God's servant.

Herod *(claps)* Oh, very good, very good indeed. You have a resonant voice, a commanding delivery. I might even give you a turn at my birthday feast tomorrow. A change from the inevitable dancers and acrobats. *(he strikes a pose)* Ladies and gentlemen! By popular request – straight from his watery success in the Jordan Valley – your very own John the Baptist! . . . But what would you do, I wonder? Tell our fortunes? A few simple conjuring tricks? What about dietary hints? That would be more in your line, wouldn't it? I believe you're quite an expert on desert cuisine. What was it – locusts and honey? Yes, locusts and honey. Not quite what my honoured guests will be used to. Certainly not Herodias. *(he moves to the bars and looks out before turning his head back towards John)* Not one of your biggest fans, Herodias. She wants me to kill you – did you know that, John the Baptist? *(walks back to stand behind John)* And you can hardly blame her, can you? Saying that her marriage is illegal, displeasing to God? *(pause)* Should I kill you? What do you think?

John You would have no power to kill me unless it had been given to you from above.

Herod Oh, very good. A truly philosophical response. You see, that's what I like about you, Baptist. You're not the run-of-the-mill kind of revolutionary. There's something about you. *(moves away)* And the people like you, don't they? Even though you're hard on them. Even though you call them to repent and be baptised. They still like you. But they don't like me. Why is that, Baptist? *(John remains silent, head down. Frustrated and annoyed, Herod moves quickly to John and pushes his head back to force him to look up)* Why is that? Answer me, damn you.

John *(slowly puts his hand on Herod's arm and pulls it away)* Because you are God's enemy, Tetrach, and I am God's messenger. That is why.

Herod God's messenger! So you keep telling me. But God doesn't seem to be looking after his messenger, does he? Else why would you be here?

John *(stands and faces Herod. He laughs)* Because my work is done, Herod. I am just the messenger, the herald, the harbinger. Announcing the arrival, preparing the ground, clearing the way. And now that he has come, my work is done. I must decrease. He must increase.

Herod Not that old story again. The Messiah. The Anointed One. The King of the Jews. A pack of lies, Baptist. There will be no new king to save the people from Roman rule. To bring down my family's kingdoms. My father put an end to that little idea once and for all.

John Your father did not succeed, Herod Antipas. *(angry)* Do you really think that you and your pathetic dynasty could stop the plans of the most high God? *(calmer)* No. Jesus survived that monstrous blood-letting and is now going about his work. The one of whom I spoke so many times. The Coming One. The one who will baptise with the Holy Spirit and with fire. The one whose sandals I am not worthy to undo – and yet, *(he is lost in thought)* and yet he allowed me to baptise him. Me, who leapt in my mother's womb when I sensed his nearness. The Christ is here, Tetrach. And he is about his business. The blind receive their sight, the lame walk, the lepers are cleansed, the deaf hear, the dead are raised. Have you not heard? Do you not yet understand? God has come to his people and the world will never be the same again. *(pause)* And my work is done. *(he returns to his bench)*

Herod You're mad, Baptist. You and that half-crazed cousin of yours. God has come to his people, indeed. The only thing to come to his people has been Roman rule and my father's family. And there's nothing you can do about it. *(he moves to the door and calls)* Open up, guard!

Guard *(enters)* Ready to leave, Excellency?

Herod More than ready. *(he turns back to speak to John)* Goodbye, Baptist. Don't forget, it's my birthday tomorrow. I might even send you in a glass of wine. Oh, no, I forgot – you don't drink, do you? But there again, I might invite you up to meet the guests. Suitably chained, of course. Herodias would like that. *(sarcastic laugh as he exits. Sound of door being locked. Laughter continues and dies away)*

John stares straight ahead as at the beginning.

Blackout.

Fourth Sunday of Advent

Marriage Guidance

This Sunday hovers on the brink of Christmas and church services are already bathed in a festive glow of carols and cribs. But in Bethlehem there are still many months to the Roman census; there is room at the inn and only animals occupy its draughty stable. In Nazareth two of the key figures of the Christmas story are filled with apprehension and doubt as the parts they are to play begin to sink into their consciousness. This simple two-hander intertwines the thoughts of Mary and Joseph as Christ's first coming draws closer.

Bible source Luke 1:26-56; Matthew 1:18-25

Performance time Six minutes

Characters Mary
Joseph

Scene setter *A blank acting space*

Mary and Joseph enter from opposite sides and move to the front of the acting space, remaining far left and right respectively. If each can be spotlit against a dim background, so much the better. As the action progresses they gradually move towards the centre until at the end they are standing together. They address the audience.

Mary I couldn't believe it when the messenger came. All in white and with this glow on his face – like something from another world. In the scrolls they read in the synagogue it says that Sarah, Abraham's wife, had a visitor like that. He said that she was going to have a baby – even though she was well past child-bearing. She laughed.

Joseph I couldn't believe it when the messenger came in the dream. All in white and with this kind of glow on his face – like something from another world. I don't dream much usually – too tired after a long day at the workbench; but this was special. It was so real – like I'm seeing you now, that's how real it was.

Mary I didn't laugh. I was too frightened. Wouldn't you be? A messenger from God telling me I was going to have a child – and me still engaged to be married! I'm a good girl; I've never been with a man – not like some of the others. And then he said that this child was going to be really special. What was it exactly? *(thinks)* Oh yes, the Son of the Most High. He was going to have *(she thinks again)* David's throne and – er – reign over the house of Jacob for ever. What else? Oh yes, his kingdom would never end. No wonder I was frightened. It just seemed like a dream.

Joseph Of course, we know all about God speaking through dreams in the scrolls. Jacob and Jeremiah and Samuel – God spoke to them in dreams – and Joseph and Daniel were able to say what other people's dreams meant. But I didn't need an interpreter for this dream – it was sort of straight from the shoulder if you like. Although I did wonder whether it was – what do they call it? – oh yes, stress-related. Because I *had* been worrying about Mary – worrying a lot.

Mary It set me worrying no end – as you can imagine, even though he tried to calm me down. 'Don't be afraid Mary,' he said. 'God has chosen you to be the mother of his Son.' I replied, 'That's what I'm worried about. I'm still a virgin, so how is *that* going to work?' Well, then he explained how God's Holy Spirit would be involved – I couldn't imagine how – and then the biggest problem came and hit me like a thunderbolt: what was I going to tell Joseph?

Joseph When she told me I just couldn't believe my ears. Pregnant, and by the Holy Spirit of God! I just didn't know what to think. I mean, she'd always seemed a good, God-fearing girl, and I know I wasn't the greatest catch under the sun being that much older, but I had a good, steady trade and – pregnant by the Holy Spirit! It knocked me back, I can tell you. Every day from then on was a nightmare. Marry her or break the engagement? I couldn't think straight. Stress? Let me tell you about it.

Mary He tried to calm me down by talking about my cousin, Elizabeth, and how she was six months pregnant – at her age. This was also God's work apparently, just like with Sarah. Well, in the end I had to accept it. I believe in God – I always have – and if that was his will, who was I to contradict it? Then he was gone and it was all over. At the time it seemed to go on for ever but it was just seconds really, like those dreams you have just before you wake up in the morning.

Joseph So when the dream came it was really an answer to prayer. I've never prayed much on my own – in the synagogue, of course, with the rest of the men – but never much on my own. But this time I did – because I didn't know what to do. If I ended the engagement, what would become of Mary? If I didn't, what sort of marriage could we have? Perhaps it could be done quietly, without too much fuss, without making her a public disgrace. About the same time her family sent her up country to visit her cousin Elizabeth and her husband Zechariah – good man, a priest, you know – so it gave me a little thinking space. And then the dream came.

Mary I told Joseph – eventually – but how do you explain to your fiancé that you're expecting a baby and it's not his? He said he needed time to think and I went off to see Elizabeth. The family thought it was a good idea and I was able to get away from all those awkward silences with Joseph. And while I was away it all seemed to fall into place. Elizabeth knew all about it – I don't know exactly how – and I felt completely happy with the whole idea. I felt I could just praise God and leave everything in his hands, whatever would happen in the future.

Joseph The messenger in the dream just confirmed everything that Mary had told me. It all seemed to fall into place. And this birth of God's Son would fulfil the words of Isaiah: 'The virgin shall conceive and bear a son.' It would all be part of God's plan. So who was I to take offence? I felt I could just leave everything in God's hands, whatever would happen in the future. And as soon as Mary got back from Elizabeth's I told her about the dream. We got married and waited for the birth of God's Son.

Mary When I got back from Elizabeth's, Joseph told me that he had a message from God in a dream and everything was going to be all right! We got married and waited for the birth of God's Son.

By now Joseph and Mary are side by side and holding hands.

Joseph Oh, one thing I forgot to say about the dream was that God's messenger told me what to call the baby.

Mary Did I say that the messenger told me what to call the baby? Well, he did.

Both We are to call him Jesus.

Blackout.

Christmas Day

The Surprise Breakfast

For most families, breakfast on Christmas Day is something of an early pit stop in the accelerating race that started with bulging stockings in the cold light of dawn and won't come to an end until the last party game has been played, the last chocolate snowman devoured and the last ball of wrapping paper binned. The church service may well be just one more lap of that familiar track but at its heart is the amazing fact that 2000 or so years ago, in some kind of Middle-Eastern hostelry, the assorted guests were sitting down to *their* breakfast unaware that God's Son was lying in a feeding trough in the stable block. This is their story, intended to fill a short space in the Christmas Day family service.

Bible source Luke 2:1-20; Isaiah 9:2, 6, 7; John 1:1-14

Performance time Six minutes

Characters
Reuben Matthews – elderly, God-fearing
Widow Jacobs – middle-aged, well-off
Adam Samuels – a lawyer; young, businesslike
Rebecca Solomon – a young mother; flustered
Isaac – her son
Ruth – her daughter
Rachel – a servant

Scene setter *The communal breakfast table in a Bethlehem inn. Use outsize painted cardboard props for marmalade and honey jars, cereal packets, crockery, etc. (a useful Sunday School/Junior Church project during the previous weeks) or simply mime with a bare table. Four seats facing the audience and one at each end. Use modern clothes; this will help to bring the message closer to the audience.*

Rachel is putting the finishing touches to the table as Reuben enters stage left, carrying a newspaper.

Reuben Good morning! That's what I like to see – a pristine breakfast table.

Rachel Oh, good morning, sir. Yes, you're the first one down this morning. I expect the others will be here shortly. *(as Reuben decides where to sit)* Why don't you sit here, sir? *(she pulls out the chair at the right-hand end)* Not so crowded.

Reuben Well, yes, I will. A thousand thanks. *(he sits and makes himself comfortable)* And who are the others?

Rachel The others? Let's see. *(ticking them off on her fingers)* You're in number six, aren't you? Well, next to you in number four is the Widow Jacobs. *(confidentially)* Not short of a bob or two, if you ask me. Then in number four there's Mr Samuels – he's a lawyer, you know. Very bright, they do say. On the other side of the corridor I'm in number three and then there's a Mrs Solomon and her two children in number five. Here for the census, I think, like yourself.

Reuben Very good, very good. An excellent resumé, my dear. *(he opens his paper but has another thought)* Tell me, did you hear a noise during the night?

Rachel A noise? Can't say I did. But then after a day in this place I go out like a light. What sort of noise?

Reuben It sounded like singing. But singing such as I've never heard in my life.

Rachel Singing? We certainly get a few songs in the bar before chucking-out time but not the sort I'm sure you'd like to hear, sir! *(they laugh)* Anyway, what can I get you for breakfast?

Reuben Oh, just some scrambled egg, I think. And brown toast and coffee. That will do nicely.

Rachel Right you are, sir. Help yourself to cereal and juice. *(she exits right)*

Reuben takes cereal, milk and juice and then, hands together, closes his eyes in prayer. Widow Jacobs enters left.

Widow Jacobs *(taking hold of second chair from left)* Don't let me interrupt you. I would never come between a man and his God – as I said to my poor dear husband many times.

Reuben Forgive my rudeness, madam. I didn't hear you come in. Here, please, allow me. *(he moves along the table and helps the widow into her chair)*

Widow Jacobs Thank you. I rejoice to see that civility is not yet dead – as my poor dear husband used to say.

Rachel enters right with plate and cup which she sets before Reuben.

Rachel Here we are, sir. Scrambled egg, brown toast and coffee.

Reuben Many thanks indeed, my dear.

Rachel *(to Widow Jacobs)* And the same for you, madam?

Widow Jacobs Good heavens, no. It would go straight to my hips. No, just a little fruit juice will suffice. *(she pours herself a glass as Adam enters left carrying a sheaf of papers. He sits down quickly)*

Adam *(to Rachel)* Porridge, kippers, wholemeal toast and black coffee. And mind it's freshly brewed. The stuff you brought me yesterday tasted like dishwater. *(he immerses himself in his papers)*

Rachel Our coffee is always fresh, sir. *(moving off right)* Dishwater indeed! Who does he think he is!

Reuben *(to Adam)* Good morning! *(silence)* I said good morning, young man.

Adam I heard you – old man.

Reuben And you didn't reply?

Widow Jacobs Just like my poor dear husband.

Adam *(without looking up)* I've no time for small talk. I have a case to defend at court this morning. Very important client. Could be the making of me. Time is money.

Reuben Of course, of course. *(pause)* Tell me, did either of you hear any singing during the night?

Widow Jacobs Singing? Oh no. I always sleep with my ear plugs in. Shuts out the world completely, you see. Allows one to concentrate on oneself.

Rachel enters from right with Adam's meal and puts it down in front of him, disturbing his papers.

Adam I was far too busy to hear any singing. Mind what you're doing, girl! I have to rely on these documents in court! *(he tuts and fusses as Rebecca comes in left, flustered)*

Rachel Why, Mrs Solomon! Is something the matter?

Rebecca You haven't seen the children, have you, Rachel? I can't find them anywhere.

Rachel Why, bless your heart, they came through the kitchen half an hour ago. They've gone out to the stable block to see the animals. I'll tell them you're here. *(she goes out right)*

Rebecca *(pulls out the chair next to Adam and sits down)* Children! It's impossible to keep track of them. My husband's coming down from Jerusalem to meet us for the registration and we're already behind time. *(to Widow Jacobs)* You know what's it like.

Widow Jacobs Fortunately my poor dear husband and I didn't have to concern ourselves with children.

Reuben *(to Rebecca)* But I know just what you mean, madam. I have seven grand-children and I can never keep up with them. I'm Reuben Matthews, by the way. This is Mrs Jacobs and that's Mr Samuels, the lawyer.

Widow Jacobs He's busy.

Reuben Can I just ask you, madam – did you happen to hear any singing in the middle of the night?

Adam Give it a rest, old man. You've got singing on the brain.

Rebecca I can't say I did; I was sorting out the clothes and making lists for most of the night. But the children were going on about some singing. In the sky, they said. And something about a bright light. Just one of their stories!

Reuben A bright light? Why, that's what I thought . . . But it can't be . . .

Ruth and Isaac run in from right, highly excited, followed by Rachel.

Isaac Mother! There's a baby in the stables.

Ruth And we were allowed to hold him!

Isaac And he was only born last night!

Ruth And they've put him in one of the feeding troughs!

Rebecca Well, that's probably a very good place. I put you in an empty drawer when you were born. Now sit down and eat your breakfast and be quick about it. We have to meet your father in half an hour.

(The children sit next to Reuben and begin eating cereal and juice hurriedly as does Rebecca)

Reuben You say there's a new baby? In the stables?

Isaac Yes. His mum and dad are with him. They're here for the census like us.

Reuben And do you know the baby's name?

Ruth Oh yes. It's Jesus.

Reuben Jesus. Saviour. Then it *is* true. For to us a child is born, to us a son is given; and the government will be upon his shoulder, and his name will be called 'Wonderful Counsellor, Mighty God, Everlasting Father, Prince of Peace'.

As Reuben is speaking everyone looks at him with expressions of interest, amazement, incomprehension or suspicion.

Rebecca Come along, children, we have to go. *(she hustles them off left)*

Reuben *(calling after them)* Keep listening for the singing, children.

Adam Is that the time? Get me a taxi, girl. *(as Rachel hesitates) Now,* please! *(they leave left)*

Widow Jacobs Well, as my poor dear husband used to say, 'Time to be off.' A little retail therapy today, I think. *(she catwalks off left)*

Reuben is lost in thought.

Reuben Goodbye. Goodbye. Singing and a bright light. His name is Jesus. But a stable and a feeding trough! Who would have thought it? *(stands and turns towards the right)* I think I had better see this baby for myself. *(he walks slowly off left)*

Ephiphany

Reunion

The Magi tread on the coat-tails of Christmas, bringing a mystical symbolism to the homespun familiarity of shepherds and stable and manger. They also, of course, spark the blood-letting that is to turn the Holy Family into refugees. The meaning of the wise men and their gifts can too easily be over-elaborated, but the one message that shines from this story like the Epiphany star itself is that from his birth the Christ Child came to earth for the Gentiles as well as the Jews. This sketch, like T. S. Eliot's *Journey of the Magi,* looks at the events of Matthew's Gospel in retrospect, pushing the Christmas narrative fast forward to Easter's bloodied cross and glorious tomb.

Bible source Matthew 2:1-12; 16-18

Performance time Five minutes

Characters Melchior – a diplomat; reserved, deep
Caspar – a scientist; down-to-earth, brusque
Balthasar – an academic; impractical, loquacious
Club servant

Scene setter *A gentlemen's club. Three chairs (low armchairs if possible or, if not, church/hall chairs with drapes) are grouped round a low table carrying half-empty glasses and a wine bottle. The three men are smartly suited. Melchior sits centre, facing the audience, Caspar and Balthasar on either side. Caspar is reading a newspaper, Balthasar drinking. The atmosphere throughout the sketch is of three professional acquaintances who at times poke fun at each other in a bantering way but are never aggressive.*

Caspar *(folding up the paper and putting it down)* I still can't believe it. Dead and buried. And after such expectation, such promise.

Balthasar Yes, but in the long march of history what is the death of one mere mortal – slave or poet, peasant or king? 'We should all be prepared', as Plato says, 'to fly away from earth to heaven as quickly as we can.'

Caspar But was he a king? It was a pretty unlikely birthplace for a king of the Jews. A sort of cave round the back of that pub. The parents showed it to us if you remember.

Balthasar Oh, don't remind me, Caspar. I have seldom been so disappointed at the outcome of a journey. And to think of what we went through to get there! Those villages – ugh!

Caspar Yes, we know you like your home comforts, Balthasar. You're better off in academia. But was he a king? What do you think, Melchior?

Melchior *(who has been lost in thought)* A king? Yes, we had the evidence, didn't we? Or did we?

Caspar *(laughs)* The perfect diplomat's answer. Did we or didn't we? Well, if you ask me, we did. The evidence was there. I'm just a practical physicist and if the evidence says take a trip and you'll find a king, I'll do it.

Balthasar Oh, yes, Caspar, we know how practical you can be.

Caspar Just as well I was. If I hadn't arranged the transport and the security and the provisions, we'd never have left Babylon, let alone reached Judea.

Melchior And Herod might never have killed those children.

Caspar No. But that's – life, isn't it? You launch an experiment, *(he motions to Melchior)* you negotiate a treaty, *(he motions to Balthasar)* you begin a debate. You have no idea where it will end.

Balthasar Perhaps that's what it was, all the time. An experiment. God decrees the birth of a king. We are sent as, what, witnesses, confirmers of the event. The child grows, becomes a man, works – so we are led to understand – miracles of healing. Is hailed as a great teacher, a prophet, the promised Messiah of the Jewish race, but, in the way of the world, fails to achieve his kingship, falls foul of the authorities and is executed. End of the experiment.

But we must not criticise God in this. As Plato says, 'The blame is his who chooses; God is blameless.'

Melchior You know, I felt that, even then. When we were in that house, kneeling on the dirt floor while the servants brought in those gifts fit for a king – the gold, the myrrh, the frankincense – I looked at the child and his mother and saw – death – as if a naked sword was hanging over that place, not a star.

Caspar Your trouble, Melchior, is that you've too much imagination. No, as Balthasar says, it was probably an experiment that failed. Happens to me all the time. *(laughter)*

Balthasar You know, one thing I've never been able to explain satisfactorily is why *we* were sent – that is, if we *were* sent, of course. Gentiles going to the Jewish nation to, as it were, reveal their king. Surely they could have done that for themselves?

Caspar Perhaps we were just being used as a, what, a kind of catalyst – a way of showing what his own people could not see for themselves?

Melchior You may be right, Caspar. Although I suppose it's all hypothetical now. What we did and who we saw and what it all meant seems to be irrelevant in the circumstances. Even so, I can't really believe that this is the end.

The waiter approaches from stage right, cloth over one arm, newspaper under the other.

Waiter Excuse me, gentlemen. Your table's ready now.

Balthasar *(rising)* Excellent. I'm anxious to see if the shoulder of lamb is as good as you say it is, Melchior.

Caspar *(rising)* Absolutely. Talking always gives me an appetite. *(to Melchior)* As Plato says! *(they laugh as Balthasar shakes his head).* Coming?

Melchior No, you two go ahead. I'll just finish my wine. I won't be long.

Caspar and Balthasar move off stage right, talking. Melchior sits thoughtfully for a moment as the waiter hovers.

Waiter Excuse me, sir. I thought you might like this evening's paper. *(he offers it)*

Melchior Oh, thank you very much. Most kind. *(he takes the paper and begins to scan the front page).* What's this! It can't be! Surely not, but . . . *(rising from the chair, visibly excited)* yes, of course! It had to be that way! Why didn't we see it? Blind, blind! *(he walks quickly off right)* Caspar! Balthasar! Wait! He's alive!

Blackout.